T0339651

Storytelling for Sustainability

Deepening the Case for Change

Jeff Leinaweaver

www.jeffleinaweaver.com
www.globalzensustainability.com
email: jeff@global-zen.com
Twitter: @globalzen

 **Routledge**
Taylor & Francis Group

LONDON AND NEW YORK

First published 2015 by Greenleaf Publishing Limited

Published 2017 by Routledge
2 Park Square, Milton Park, Abingdon, Oxon OX14 4RN
711 Third Avenue, New York, NY 10017, USA

Routledge is an imprint of the Taylor & Francis Group, an informa business

ISBN 978-1-910174-50-0 (pbk)

A catalogue record for this title is available from the British Library.

Page design and typesetting by Alison Rayner
Cover by Becky Chilcott

Abstract

IN THE WORLDS OF STRATEGIC SUSTAINABILITY, corporate social responsibility and social change, more and more attention is being focused on the importance of storytelling as a key component in one's toolkit for change. In this Dō Short, we'll explore which stories and ways of storytelling lead to success and which ways lead to failure. Readers will develop a sense of why the ancient human practice of storytelling is relevant today as a key skill for influencing and shaping a better and more sustainable world. We will also explore through some practical exercises how to become better storytellers in order to communicate, advocate, educate, organize, and transmit resonance and relational authenticity. *Storytelling for Sustainability: Deepening the Case for Change* offers a comprehensive primer on storytelling as a whole-brain practice, where storytelling is as much an intrapreneurial exercise as it is an approach to strategic communication and social change.

About the Author

DR JEFF LEINAWEAVER is a storyteller, sustainability strategist, writer and educator who blends the power of storytelling and the practice of narrative leadership into the fields of corporate social responsibility, organizational development, sustainability reporting and permaculture design. Jeff has published widely, including in academic journals, The Associated Press, *The Guardian*'s sustainability business column and others. Jeff is managing partner at Global Zen Sustainability and a leading GRI-certified trainer consultant for ISOS CSR and Associate for The Natural Step US. Jeff is also a graduate faculty member in sustainability and MBA program at the Bainbridge Graduate Institute at Pinchot, the University of Washington, Antioch University and Capella. He has been a communication fellow at the CMM Institute for Personal and Social Evolution and Fielding Graduate University's Institute for Social Innovation. As a performing storyteller, Jeff has been a featured teller at the National Storytelling Network Conference, the Northwest Folklife Festival and throughout the United States and Canada. His latest storytelling album, *Wild Minds in Uncertain Times*, is available on iTunes and **http://www.cdbaby.com/cd/jeffleinaweaver**

Acknowledgments

A **NUMBER OF INDIVIDUALS** helped provide counsel and support in preparation for this book. I could not have done this without the support, advice and encouragement of Melanie Bigalke, who also helped in creating the graphics. In addition, I appreciate the feedback and wise insight from Alice MacGillivray, Marilyn Price-Mitchell, Jennifer Pontzer, Anne Acosta, Zach Bigalke, Rob Dalton, Tamara Gordy and my wife Joanna. I would also like to dedicate this book to my mentor and friend, Barnett Pearce – here's to making better social and sustainable worlds through the stories we tell!

Contents

Introduction

THE STORIES WE TELL MATTER. Every person, every community, every place has a story. Stories shape our identities, our imagination, each other and how we know the world around us. Humans are storytelling animals.

To change our world, we need to change our stories. It has always been this way. Since the days of our earliest ancestors, our ability to tell, listen to and remember story has been our key skill and conduit for knowledge sharing, communication, expression and most importantly, survival. Such is the case of storytelling for sustainability.

Consider Annie Leonard's critically acclaimed *Story of Stuff*[1] which started as a personal passion and grew into a fun, short animated documentary story about the lifecycle of material goods. This story went from being 'just a story' to become a global phenomenon, a movement and a non-profit organization. Annie Leonard told the story behind humanity's trance of consumerism and exposed how our cultural story is driving the 'need' for more and more stuff. Beyond entertainment, the *Story of Stuff* is, if anything, a survival story, a sustainability story and a plea to wake up and stop telling a story of unsustainability. If we don't, we won't survive; we'll run out of stuff.

This book, *Storytelling for Sustainability: Deepening the Case for Change*, is about the stories we tell, as much as it is about the person, community or organization telling the stories. This is also a book about how to re-see story, and like the *Story of Stuff*, a book to teach us to recognize that sometimes we have learned to tell the wrong stories, well.

Tell me a fact and I'll learn. Tell me a truth and I'll believe. But tell me a story and it will live in my heart forever. INDIAN PROVERB[2]

What's tricky about 'story' and 'storytelling' is that it's inherently invisible. Story is an intangible thing with many interpretations of what 'is' story and what 'is' storytelling. Regardless of how one approaches storytelling, the challenge is to understand how to make the invisible visible, to make story more tangible, valuable and more impactful towards behavior change, which includes changing belief systems as well as organizational systems.

To develop one's storytelling toolkit, you'll learn ways to make story more visible and more tangible. We'll explore which stories and ways of storytelling lead to success and which stories lead to failure, specifically highlighting three patterns of storytelling communication: *fact telling*, *story selling* and *storytelling*. I will also introduce a storytelling model called the *Triple-Storyline* model of storytelling sustainability that explores the storytelling elements of person, people and place.

We'll also discuss why the ancient human practice of storytelling is relevant today, why there's a call to rekindle one's storytelling instinct, and how it relates to why people are called to become change agents and do sustainability work.

The most influential sustainability professionals and change agents are those who can go beyond metrics and tap into something deeper, more essential, through story. People ask for data, but they believe stories. People want real, messy, untold stories, imaginative tales – tangible change doesn't happen through shallow stories, infotainment, mind-numbing sustainability reports or greenwashing. Change only happens when we're convinced by the intangible and undeniable truth told through a story. This book is an approach to deep green storytelling, a holistic approach to storytelling for sustainability.

Even though the focus of this book is not about brand storytelling, strategic marketing and persuasive presentations, the ideas and practices in this book can add meaning, depth and authenticity to these efforts. At a personal and professional level, the ideas, stories, questions and exercises in this book will help you become a better storyteller and influencer. You'll develop a mindful capacity for narrative leadership. Along the way, you will also learn the basic mechanics of what makes a story, how to critically think about story, and why this is important to your storytelling efforts for sustainability.

Additionally, throughout this book, sections of our conversation will be interspersed with a retelling of the fairy tale 'The Frog Prince'.[3] My intention behind the retelling of a simple fairy tale is to offer up a 'mything link' in our conversation on storytelling and sustainability – a perspective beyond the limits of a literal interpretation or specific method for organizational intervention or individual leadership, and rather as an invitation and provocation of one's intuitive imagination, along with a moment for reflection on a story within a story. After all, our imagination may be the greatest X-factor for change and our ability to flip the script on the story of an unsustainable world.

Most importantly, the more you work with, muse and reflect upon the questions, practices and ideas found in this book, the more you will get out of it, and the more development you will see of yourself as storyteller.

To become a better storyteller, and influence change, you must dive in and do it, telling and listening to more stories at every level. The path of the storyteller can be a curious and ever-rewarding rabbit hole to fall into. Remember, in order to advocate, educate, organize and communicate about the stories that matter, storytelling for sustainability begins with you!

CHAPTER 1

What Makes a Story a Story

Once upon a time ...

ONCE UPON A TIME, in the not-so-distant past of the greater human story, there was no television and no Internet. There were no smartphones or even books. All we had was story. Communication, entertainment, collective knowledge – story was central to the human experience and for survival. Oral stories were passed from one to another on the bridge of breath, from person to person, ancestor to ancestor. The stories told spanned all creation and helped humanity communicate and share knowledge, influence decision-making, entertain, dream and ultimately help us make sense of the worlds around us, both seen and unseen.

A hero is someone who has given his or her life to something bigger than oneself. JOSEPH CAMPBELL[4]

With storytelling central to both individual and community in such a concrete way, being a successful storyteller – and story listener – was a prized and important survival skill for personal and community 'sustainability'. It is no wonder, then, that there was a common ancient belief that, despite the hardship and challenges of actually living and surviving on a day-to-day basis, the world could only end if all the stories came to an end at the same time. Sitting by the campfire, telling stories, and looking up at the stars was not an optional activity, but key to our longevity as individuals and as part of a greater human tribe.

WHAT MAKES
A STORY A STORY

Our storytelling ancestors were wise. They recognized that there are gene-rally three types and/or levels of stories ongoing in the world at all times:

- The *big or mythic stories* that helped make sense of the mystery of life, appealing to our sense of awe and wonder of being.

- The *middle stories* that shape civilization, give image to our gods, explain how power works, how the world ought to be, and how our culture shapes our collective sense of 'the normal'.

- The little stories – the stories of an individual life, including our own personal mythos and ongoing exploration of what fate and destiny means to us and whether or not we are living with purpose.

The old storytellers recognized that *big stories, middle stories* and *little stories* each serve an essential human function and are organic to this world. Yet these stories often co-exist and function in a way where they are all secretly connected but hidden from view, with each level of story functioning as its own repository of memory.

Because humans are naturally curious and dramatic, these storytellers understood that in order to fully live out one's own personal story in the most meaningful way, everyone in the human tribe must be challenged to search for a pathway of meaning between these three levels of ongoing storytelling. We are hardwired to search for the hero within, and therefore get into two kinds of trouble: good trouble or bad trouble. Good trouble becomes the adventures we seek, the rights we try and wrong, whereas the bad trouble becomes the issues and dragons we try to ignore, deny or dismiss, but still ends up finding us and reluctantly pulling us into the journey kicking and screaming.

HUMAN HIERARCHY OF STORIES	STORY FUNCTION	STORY LINE LEVEL
Big story	Cosmological, awe, mystery	Mythic, sacred, religious, symbolic
Middle story	Socio-cultural organizational, educational	Us & them, ancestor she, he, we, us
Little story	Individual	I am, me, and the hero within

To take this challenge, an individual is therefore called into service to something bigger than oneself. Only as a result of this process do we, as individuals, learn how we are secretly (or not) contributing to the ongoing creation of the world by searching for a pathway of meaning between these three levels of ongoing storytelling. This is why it is natural for people to see their own lives as an unfolding story and ongoing personal mythology, where we tell and retell ourselves the story about who we are and our place and purpose in the world. The retrospective process of personal narrative is our own form of memory-making and personal mythologizing. It's how we process the big questions of 'Who am I?' and 'Why am I here?' We are storytelling animals, always in search for meaning through the conduit and nourishment of story.

Now, it is not always an easy thing to do, to find the right type of trouble to get into and search for the connection between these three levels of stories. But when the tumblers fall into place and the little stories, middle stories and big stories connect, our worlds and personal narrative begin to make sense in a new way. We find connection and a deeper purpose and place. We function differently when our many different stories of self and life coalesce. We no longer fear the big mysteries, and 'what ifs' in life, but find signposts of alignment, trust and purpose in our place in the world. We often call this 'synchronicity': when all of the threads of our story intersect with a jigsaw puzzle of other narratives and events that suddenly make sense in an often compelling and unexplainable way. It's as if we receive a cosmic nod to our own ongoing mythic journeys.

This is what Joseph Campbell was also trying to communicate in speaking of a *Hero with a Thousand Faces*, and why he found it so important to sketch out a mythic map, a story pattern, of human development called the Hero's Journey.

Campbell believed that inside each person there is a mythic story that is trying to move from within an individual to live and manifest outside in the world of civilization. These mythic stories can change the world's institutions and culture, providing connection between the hero's internal story and impact upon the world.

From this point of view, each person is born into a seed story (which is our birthright, our original medicine). This story takes root over time and provides a core 'proto-story' for one's personal narrative and individual heroic journey. From this proto-story, we tell and become many stories, and eventually find ourselves in a great delta of narratives of and about ourselves. These currents and eddies of story constantly influence the story of our communities, the greater body politic, and world-at-large.

How does the story relate to our current problems of unsustainability? Why do people become sustainability professionals, activists, community

FIGURE 1. Three levels of story.

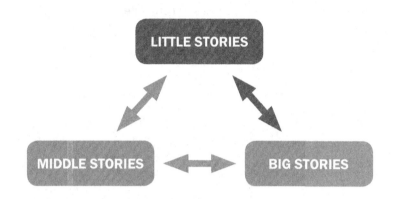

organizers, social entrepreneurs and so on? People want purpose, autonomy, right livelihood, and to work for companies and organizations that offer right alignment with their values. The story of sustainability is relevant because it is a journey of human development and change, and is not just about one meta-narrative but many stories that are told and retold in order to participate in the constant making and remaking of the world. People want to follow their bliss by getting into the right type of trouble of making change, and thereby increasing the quality of life, righting the wrongs of the world, and working to preserve whole modes of life. More than ever people want to take part in the creation of a new set of stories at individual, organizational, socio-cultural and sacred levels.

The only way we can understand how to use story as a method for change is to first understand why people are drawn to becoming change agents and sustainability as a profession. In living one's life as a storied process, people are answering the call of their own heroic journey to take part in telling the new story of 'what is' and what 'ought to be' in order meet the goal of a globally sustainable, socially just world. People do not want to be walking work-zombies or corporate shills. For employee engagement, as an example, we need to recognize this goes deeper, to how each employee feels aligned with his or her own sense of purpose and heroic story.

Exercise

- What does heroic mean to you in regards to sustainability?

- How did you get interested in sustainability and change work?

- How does your passion for sustainability tie into your own personal life story and personal mythos?

- What does it mean to follow one's calling?

The hero's challenge, and our own, is to explore the function and meaning between these three levels of ongoing storytelling and our own proto-story in order to more consciously live out the story of our lives. As storytellers of our own lives, we are the heroes we've been waiting for on this sustainability journey. Our 'once upon a time' moment is now, and our call to adventure is to take part in the active telling of the sustainability story.

What's in a story?

From prehistoric cave drawings to old fairy tales like 'The Frog Prince' to water-cooler gossip, there are as many ways to tell a story as there are stories. But just what makes a story?

STORYTELLING FOR SUSTAINABILITY: DEEPENING THE CASE FOR CHANGE

....

Half the art of storytelling [is] to keep a story free from explanation.
WALTER BENJAMIN, THE STORYTELLER[5]

....

Many say a story is simply a collection of five basic elements, real or fictitious, which are strung together in a linear sequence between a beginning, middle and end. These five elements include the setting, characters, plot, conflict and resolution.

There are others who say that there is a sixth hidden element. Held within a story there is always a 'pastness' or memory of how these five elements hold together as one whole story. Memory is the sixth and possibly most important element to what's in a story, and to the storytelling process. Memory is an intangible factor to what's in a story. And, it is in the immediacy of assembling these five elements, by memory, where we find ourselves storying the story. This makes story unique to each telling. This is also why no two tellers will tell the same story the same way twice – even if it's understood to be the same story! Consider the tradition of oral narrative, where memory was the only container for story and all human knowledge. Every time a story was told, it was both about the past, the present moment and the future. In oral cultures, it is considered a huge responsibility to be a keeper of story, to be a storyteller.

While we no longer live in a strictly oral narrative world, the element of memory in story still exists, often in taken-for-granted and everyday ways. Think of something simple, like a group of people witnessing a minor car accident. The police, and possibly lawyers, will want to hear people's stories. The event happens, but it is in the reassembly of the events of the accident in each person's memory that makes the story similar or different when told. In this we can see the relative nature of stories, and

FIGURE 2. The elements of story.

why it's common to have many conflicting stories told about a single event, such as a car accident.

This is also why any story is often said to be a dynamic equation: {fact + fiction = faction}. In part this is because memory is human and therefore malleable over time, subject to re-calling the elements of a story differently. Memory impacts the role of time and how we account for this in our stories. Now consider the complexity of telling the sustainability story. It is a story that is as exponential and variable as the human population.

I like to think of this simply – story is what's being made and shaped in the now, and narrative is the sharing of the memory of what happened with the other five elements. Story and narrative are two sides of the same coin.

What is storytelling?

Everyone has a story to tell, and while we could spend a lifetime learning the art and technique of storytelling, for most of us it's the simple telling or hearing of a story that's important. Stories matter when told with the right intent, at the right time and place: this is storytelling. After all, if story is memory, there is a need for storytelling to have an ethic of authenticity.

Storytelling is not about perfected performance, it is much more 'open-mic' and has a need for a teller, a willing listener and a willing story. Storytelling is not about the storyteller. It's not an opportunity to

Thoughts to ponder ...

- Ask yourself, what do you see are the important qualities of a well-told story?

- How does your sense of place influence your storytelling?

- What does a well-told story mean within an organizational or professional context?

- When you are working with others what do you 'do' with the story you tell, what's the intent behind how you share and tell story?

monologue about a story or debate facts of another's story. Storytelling is being present, in the moment, engaged in listening, being reflective and sharing, not being talked at, or talking at an issue.

What makes storytelling different is that it exists in a continuum between communication and communion – where it is equally an event or ritual as much a method of communication. Storytelling can be as much a practice of entertainment or business currency as it is a sacred human act. Indeed, story is much more than its six elements – setting, characters, plot, conflict, resolution and the memory or knowing of the story.

Storytelling is about a coordinated management of meaning between the storyteller, the listener and the story itself. This is most often referred to as the storytelling triangle – where story lives in a space between teller and listener. It is also why 'story' has its own X-factor: story is a black box that is subject to the storyteller's interpretation, ethic, imagination, relativity and mystery in meaning.

FIGURE 3. Storytelling triangle.

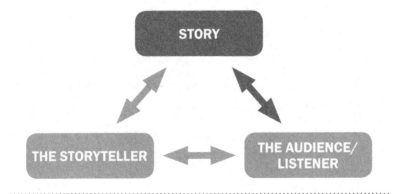

Image and the shape of storytelling

From cave art and storyboards, to live performances and video game stories, storytelling is primarily a practice in first working with image and shape, before moving to words and language. Why? Quite simply because image and shape hold memory and meaning better than words and language. It is also easer to remember a story through image, and share a story through metaphor. The storytelling triangle is just one shape of many that help us be better storytellers.

The author and iconoclast Kurt Vonnegut[6] believed there are shapes inside stories, in part because no true story has a flat or perfect trajectory. Story is about drama, tragedy, comedy, etc. Story and storytelling naturally fluctuate between highs and lows – a continuum between happiness and sadness. This is what makes story so human.

Vonnegut believed stories could be graphed along an X–Y axis of good fortune and ill fortune. By seeing the shape and image inside a story,

....

FIGURE 4. Storyline graph (blank).

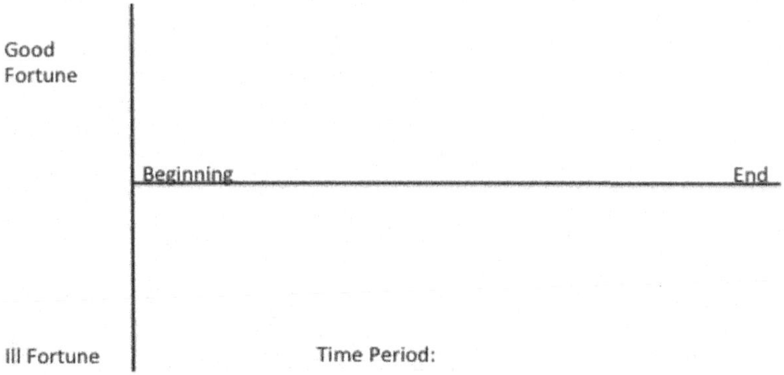

patterns emerge and we can better predict and understand the stories we tell, develop insight into our storytelling and learn why some stories work and why others don't, and why. We will explore the shape and graph of story throughout the book.

One of the biggest mistakes people make in trying to tell better stories is going to the words of the story first. Too many people try to tell perfect stories, overly literal tellings, tightly controlled by the exact words. Quite often this is a recipe for two-dimensional, uninspired, overly formulaic recitations of a story. People tell shallow stories, where as an example every story has to be rags-to-riches, or a storyline that moves from bad to good. If you don't allow a story to breathe, and have the natural ups and downs of real story, the storytelling flatlines. People tune out. It has the odor of inauthenticity.

FIGURE 5. Storyline graph – inauthentic story shapes.

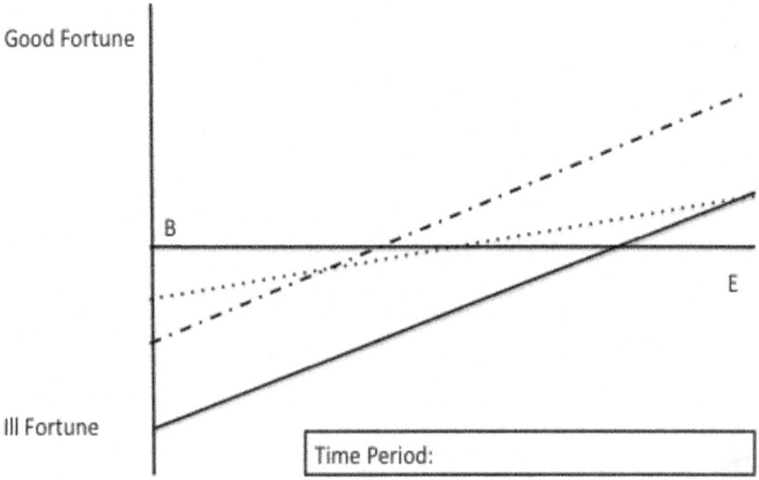

This is one of the big problems with the telling of the sustainability story – there are too many people trying to create an exact script of a new and perfect sustainability story. Think of many corporate sustainability reports, which have perfectly scripted stories. Stories told to create a 'party line' about how to tell and imbibe the story. This is not always a successful effort. We all have to have our own images of this sustainability/ unsustainability story. We must learn how to tell our stories in a way that they can scale and flex between our individual selves, organizational selves and cultural selves.

Drawing on the inner images of a story, you allow your story to breathe through you as the storyteller. Sometimes in your memory, different images show up which require you to use different words for telling the story. Through practice, you develop an ability to trust yourself and take risks in telling your stories, knowing that the inner images and memories will change depending on the story, listener and setting for your story. As a result, many of the storytelling exercises in this book are built around building up your right-brain storytelling muscle.

Developing an ability to know how to tell a story in image first, allows you to create stories that are 'loose-tight' by design, meaning that by anchoring your understanding of a story as an image and shape you can go 'off script' and expand and contract your telling as deemed appropriate to the situation. It means you may tell the same story a 100 different ways, but have it still be the same core story. The best storytellers channel the 'theatre of the mind' and the image memory of story into language, expression and body. It is in this 'tellingness' of the story that allows others to engage with the story, make it their own story, and connect themselves into the story.

Storytelling platforms

A storytelling platform is the setting, place or stage that enables you to tell your story in a particular way. Each platform will change how you tell your story. It is also the medium where you engage your audience. You can tell the same story through multiple platforms: the trick is knowing which platform serves your story the best at the time it is told. Here's a basic list of an ever-growing and fluid category.

TRADITIONAL PLATFORMS	DIGITAL & SOCIAL MEDIA
Around a fire, in nature	Recorded voice, radio, podcasting
Home	Film, video, TV
Sharing meals (anywhere)	Social media: Twitter, Facebook, Instagram, Tumblr, YouTube
Places of worship	PowerPoint, Prezi, Screencast, Webinar
Places in community: pubs, coffee shops, restaurants	Websites, blogs
Performance halls	Gaming
At work, presentations, the boardroom	Animation, visual, graphic recording
Books, magazines, newspapers	Mobile devices, phones, tablets
Brand advertising and marketing, TV	Apps
Corporate reporting and communications	Skype, Facetime, Google Hangouts, etc.

As storytellers, storytelling implores us to listen deeply to those stories around us and those stories within us to find old and new pathways between our personal stories and those big stories which help our organizations, social institutions and the world-at-large respond to an era of great change and unsustainability. In turn, as communities of storytellers, and organizations of storytellers, we are in perpetual motion around the storytelling triangle, constantly weaving our stories together.

Making story your own

How do you tell better stories? The answer is, you learn by doing. We 'do' things with story, not just tell stories.

As a way to begin, the following exercise is a great core storytelling practice in the 'doing' of story, particularly in developing your own voice and style as a storyteller. This is key for developing one's presence as a storyteller.

Core storytelling exercise: Fly on the wall

Find a story spot – any spot where you can sit relatively unnoticed and serve in the role of an observer and people watcher – this could be a coffee shop, a train station, your local library, in transit, etc. Time yourself for 15 minutes and simply observe others. Be a fly on the wall. As you watch, consider what story, or stories are unfolding in front of you. When the time is finished, complete the steps below.

- STEP 1: Either on a computer or pen to paper, time yourself for 5 minutes and either sketch out or free-write the story of what you observed as the fly on the wall. Do not describe – tell a story. Be as imaginative as you want, or as true-to-life as you feel appropriate for the story and elements that shows up.

- STEP 2: Later that day or that week, connect with someone else. Time yourself for 5 minutes and orally tell the story of what you observed as the fly on the wall. Do not describe or explain – tell a story.

Section takeaways

- Storytelling is for everyone

- Storytelling is an embodied practice

- It's about the drama of relationship between a story's inner elements

- Story exists with a will of its own, separate from the teller and listener

- Story is memory – holding image, shape and knowledge

- It's a reflection of a person, people and place

- It's holistic – offering a whole-brain translation between left-brain logic with right-brain metaphor and image

Opening to the imagination of story

I'd like to invite you, as a reader, to take a moment and be willing to take a non-traditional detour in our conversation on storytelling for sustainability by exploring the old and beloved folk tale of 'The Frog Prince'. We will explore this tale in four parts, including a visual unfolding of the story's shape.

To be better storytellers, and to influence adaptive change towards sustainability, we also need to learn how to use myth and story as a lens from which we consider our own lives, the roles of our institutions and the stories of our culture. You just might be surprised at the results of taking the time to work with and to mine a story for its gold.

It may be unorthodox for a professional or business context to be talking about 'fairy tale' stories, but because the sustainability story is in so many ways a story of the future, our capacity as storytellers is inextricably connected to our ability to use our imaginations. I believe we have to learn how to 'imaginate' the sustainability story together. After all, where does a business's future vision and mission come from? Certainly not the status quo!

For millennia, story has been used as a method of teaching and social change with groups of ordinary folks (aka folk tales). Myths and folk stories were told as parables (stories with hidden messages or teachings), in order to develop a collective capacity not only to be together and to deepen an understanding of the world, but to raise new questions, challenge old ways of being and develop an ability to imagine together, regardless of viewpoint or position in the world. Simply put, a good story provokes thought, and this creates change!

WHAT MAKES
A STORY A STORY

I've chosen 'The Frog Prince' for our conversation because this story was a core story for the famous mythologist Joseph Campbell.[7] He used this story[8] specifically to highlight some of the most inspiring, influential and powerful ideas we have today about story – 'Follow Your Bliss' and the 'Hero's Journey'. It is because of his work that we better see the relevance and connection between story, the role of change, the influence of leadership and the power of the individual quest for adventure and purpose in life. I see these ideas as core to the sustainability story and the many inner narratives and motivators for those involved with the sustainability movement.

For now, as a storyteller, I invite you to pull up a seat at the great roaring campfire of the mind and consider an old and beloved tale that may have something to say to you about this sustainability story we're trying to tell …

THE FROG PRINCE: PART 1

ONCE, LONG AGO IN A TIME LIKE OURS, there lived a king who had three beautiful daughters. The king's daughters were exceedingly lovely, but the youngest princess was so beautiful that the sun itself burned even brighter every time it shone upon her face.

Near the king's castle there was a large, dark forest, and in this forest there was an old linden tree with great gnarled roots. Nestled within the protruding roots of this old tree there was a well. When the weather was warm the princess would sneak away from her sisters and go out into the forest and sit at the edge of the cool well, leaning upon the tree to support her. To pass the time, the princess would take her beloved golden ball, throw it into the air, and catch it. She loved to sit at this well under the great tree and spend her days. It was her favorite pastime and the golden ball was her favorite toy.

One day it happened – as the princess's golden ball flew high into the air, it fell far away from her hands, and instead fell to the ground and bounced off the great tree's roots, dropping right into the water of the dark well. The princess followed it with her eyes, but the ball disappeared, and the well was so deep that she could not see its murky bottom. She began to cry, 'My beautiful golden ball is lost. What will I do? I'd give anything, if only I could get my ball back: my clothes, my precious stones, my pearls, anything in the world.'

FIGURE 6. The story and shape of The Frog Prince (Act 1).

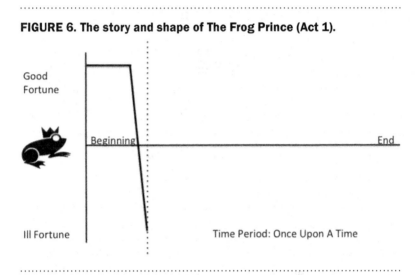

Questions to consider

Joseph Campbell used 'The Frog Prince' as his quintessential story to illustrate the hero's journey. Do you see this fairy tale as a heroic story? For many, this is a surprise. Assuming 'The Frog Prince' is also a parable, what clues does it hold in our conversation on storytelling sustainability? What surprises you in the story?

- In this opening, can you locate the six elements of story? Where is the memory?

- In everyday life, the Sun and Trees are a part of our daily life and sense of place. In this story, what roles do the Sun and the Tree play? Do you see them as objects or as quietly alive and animate?

- With all that the Sun can see, isn't it interesting that our princess would stand out?

- What would your golden ball be? What does it mean to lose it in a deep well? What would you do to get it back?

....

CHAPTER 2

Story as Maps and Mystery

Big stories matter

EVERY CULTURE HAS ITS BIG STORIES, and these stories are incredibly powerful in shaping what is possible in the world. These cultural stories can also be maladaptive, inhibiting what's possible in the world, contributing to our own dysfunction and demise. Big stories shape our imagination of what we believe is real and not real.

Consider a group of Vikings, led by Eric the Red, who set out from Norway a thousand years ago and colonized the harsh southern coast of Greenland. Deep in the safe harbor of two fjords, the colonists were able to establish a community of townships with sturdy stone structures, churches and farms. They were happy. Living mostly on traditional European livestock and grains, they traded with medieval Norway for local walrus tusks and other rare Icelandic materials. As these things go, the colonists were successful, growing to a population of about 5,000 people. This land became their home for nearly 500 years. But one day, things began to change. After a series of intensely cold winters, the mainstay of the community's diet – the livestock – began to die off. Soon more things

It's only in recent centuries that we've gotten locked into one reality – permeability and flexibility were the way of humans for 35,000 years. WERNER HERZOG, *CAVE OF FORGOTTEN DREAMS*[9]

unraveled. It got colder, they began to starve to death, social order broke down, and then suddenly the incomprehensible happened – the colony collapsed.

Things didn't have to happen this way. After all, the neighboring Inuit people, who shared the same lands, survived. The local waters were teeming with fish and had enough seals (and seal blubber) for food, heat and light. So why didn't the colonists eat the fish and follow the successful practices of the Inuit?

According to evolutionary biologist Jared Diamond,[10] the answer isn't as simple as it got cold and they died. The Vikings were killed by a cultural story, a big story, of what was 'civilized' and a story of what and who was 'uncivilized' – the Inuit. The Vikings despised the Inuit and this, in part,

FIGURE 7. Storyline (Vikings).

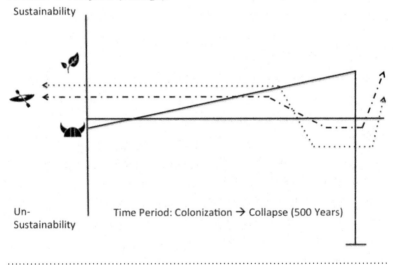

kept them from eating fish and following the sustainable practices of the Inuit. Instead, the Vikings chose to superimpose their own cultural story on the lands where they lived, recreating the colony and its stories as a mirror of their Norse heritage. They thought everything was fine until suddenly it wasn't. They got really good at telling the wrong story, well!

What's important about this story of collapse is that it's not unique. Big, maladaptive cultural stories have ranged from our Viking story to the Mayans, Olmecs, Anasazi, Easter Islanders and the Aztecs, just to name a few. In studying why societies collapse, Diamond found that cultures choose to fail or succeed by way of their cultural story of reality. Diamond attributes collapse to rigid thinking and a failure to perceive dependence on basic resources.

At a cultural and individual level, big stories operate in dynamic feedback loops, both positive and negative enforcing loops. Based on the stories a culture tells itself, Diamond believes there are five factors – five storylines if you will – that impact how we tell our big cultural stories and whether or not these stories allow us, as both individuals and members of our culture, to be adaptive and act sustainably, or whether or not we are maladaptive and unsustainable.

These factors of collapse include: 1) climate change, 2) loss of trade, 3) war with neighbors, 4) self-imposed environmental degradation and 5) political intransigence. As storylines, these factors are dynamically interconnected and complex,

Collapse-factor storylines

1. Climate change
2. Wars over resources
3. Loss of trade & business
4. Environmental degradation
5. Political intransigence

intertwining people, culture and place. From a storytelling perspective, collapse typically occurs because cultures develop blind spots to their own maladaptive narratives, like the Vikings.

Cultures fall into self-perpetuating, maladaptive feedback loops where they get really good at telling the wrong stories, well! Cultures also 'stack-rank' their storylines, creating a hierarchy of stories that define good stories vs bad stories, tellable stories vs untellable stories. It's therefore a mistake to collapse the sustainability story into just one category, such as a story about climate change. The story of sustainability encompasses all of these five collapse-factor storylines.

Also understand that storytelling for sustainability is also about telling old storylines in new ways. Telling old storylines in new ways often challenges the story of the status quo. Don't be afraid to tell the untold or untellable stories. This is what's often needed to change maladaptive, unsustainable stories. Think of the story about the Emperor's New Clothes: it's an 'innocent' folk tale that tells big social truths about the illusion of power and challenging the status quo without the use of facts.

> *I wonder how many Vikings wanted to say, why don't we eat the fish? Why don't we work with those people, the other, they seem to be doing ok? I've noticed we're overgrazing ... Why don't we help each other story a new way, and work through our differences of storylines? Why do we have to pretend we are telling a better, more civilized story, when it's the same old, habitual big story?*

I ask this in part because too often I run into change agents and sustainability professionals who tell one story publicly, a more hopeful one, but privately are more pessimistic and unsure of the future. So in many cases, we have an espoused cultural story that's told and an untold, often 'shadow', story that's going on underneath.

One of the best ways to consider our current situation is to consider how we tell the 'sustainability story'. The sustainability story is a big story, a canopy of many stories that trickles down into our own individual storylines and personal mythology.

Big stories, little stories

Mother Theresa famously said, 'If I look at the masses I will never act. If I look at the one, I will.'

Telling stories about individual people and specific moments in their lives are much more personal and powerful than those that speak broadly about big stories and sustainability issues. You need to link big stories to the little stories, telling the big story through their eyes, point of view and experiences.

In researching and writing the book *Half the Sky*,[12] Nicholas Kristoff knew the only way he could call attention to sex-trafficking and the modern slave trade was through the stories of individual women who had overcome adversity rather than succumbed to it.

Within three weeks of printing, the book became a *New York Times* bestseller and became the seed story which has started a movement and new foundation, along with an online video game and television documentary for home-based viewing parties to bring new people to the cause.

http://www.halftheskymovement.org/[13]

STORY AS
MAPS AND MYSTERY

Like the *Story of Stuff*, and the story of the Vikings, we need to know if our stories feed into and optimize bad systems. Do we take part in telling the wrong stories well? As a storyteller, telling stories with an intent, such as sustainability, we need to understand how our stories ultimately impact some future state of being because every story has an afterlife.

Probably the most common and collectively held definition of today's view of sustainability is informed by the United Nation's 1987 *Brundtland Report on Our Common Future*[11] which defines sustainability as 'development that meets the needs of the present without compromising the ability of future generations to meet their own needs'. If we accept this definition of sustainability, the challenge for storytellers is to tell a sustainability story that informs a shared and attainable vision of the future. This vision must be compelling enough to be told in the now, and compelling enough to inspire retelling by others, so that it equally informs and continues to be retold by future generations. After all, unsustainability is not a one-generation fix. We must tell and coordinate a core sustainability story that will help all of us and every generation adapt and change at an individual, organizational and a worldview level.

When you tell stories of sustainability, do you imagine and paint a picture that the future will be better, transformed by steady progress and rising human wisdom based on practices of sustainability? Or do you have a more pessimistic view of things? Do you tell a story with the next generation in mind, or just the next quarterly report? How does your story of sustainability end?

What's important to note here is that we don't know how our sustainability story is going to end, yet. It's ok not to know the future; there's wisdom in not knowing. As a storyteller, I think it's perfectly ok to make it up! That's part of the job description. Instead, we must cultivate our imagination of what's possible through the stories we tell. We have to imagine what sustainability could be. Vision quests, scenario planning, World Café dialogues and futurecasting are just some examples of ways in which we can explore these big storylines and imagine the what ifs of our sustainability/unsustainability stories.

Ultimately, what does storytelling for sustainability look like to you, your organization or community? What is your story in service to, its intent – what are you storytelling for? What stories do you wish you were brave enough to tell, but don't? What big stories do you listen to? What stories are you told to tell? In your world, what are the wrong stories being told well?

It's not easy being green:
The failure of the sustainability story

When it comes to sustainability, everyone has an opinion. We live in a time of blurred lines between fact, fiction and 'faction'. We live in a postmodern era where every voice matters, truth is relative, and each of us is able to express a point of view. Just trying to have a group of stakeholders come together around a commonly accepted definition and shared understanding of what 'sustainability' means can be a challenge.

It is no wonder that, in a time like this, we have more polarizing stories told about the 'reality' of global warming and the greater challenges to our collective existence within this sustainability story. The question is, if we can't mutually share in our stories at an individual, organizational and social level, how can we ever coordinate our efforts to story a future for the next generations, without devolving into 'Us and Them' stories? How do we avoid the fate of the Vikings?

As an example of the growing continuum of polarized storytelling, Yale's Project on Climate Change Communication[14] identified six distinct cultures of Americans who have varying belief around global warming, each with their own unique story of what's going on in the world, each with their own story of 'the other'. So despite the scientific data, and the urgency of sustainability, stories that matter to everyone may not matter if we are in poor communication with each other.

By population, America's 'Global Warming Six'[15] include: 1) the Alarmed (16%), 2) the Concerned (25%), 3) the Cautious (25%),

> *The universe is made of stories, not atoms.* **MURIEL RUKEYESER, POET**[16]

4) the Disengaged (9%), 5) the Doubtful (13%) and 6) the Dismissive (8%). The six Americas do not vary much by age, gender, race or income, but rather are stretched along a continuum of stories that express their belief, concern and engagement towards the topic of climate change, or just the opposite. These six Americas are essentially story silos, where the stories told, and heard told, emphasize espoused stories, group-think and group norms over a free-range circulation of stories (which holds a storytelling X-factor for change). So instead, we have story wars between story silos – and we have more sticks than carrots!

Adding fuel to these narrative dynamics, Yale's Climate Change Communication program also conducted additional research[17] on the role of the media and found there is a growing media and social media 'echo chamber' effect which influences and enables people to hear and tell only stories which are consistent with their own views and opinions, while simultaneously blocking stories with different points of view. When technology allows you to personalize your news, engage in social media and in your digital world, there is a potential for one to intentionally or unintentionally sort things in and out of one's life. Thus individuals become more compartmentalized and less able to deal with change.

In studying how people communicate and share stories about global warming, some of Yale's key findings were quite alarming, and included the following:

- Only one in three Americans say they discuss global warming at least occasionally with friends or family, down 8 points since November 2008.

- Few Americans (<8%) communicated publically about global warming in the past 12 months (e.g. online or in the media).

- One in four Americans discussed a company's 'irresponsible environmental behavior' with friends and/or family in the past 12 months.

- Americans say their own family and friends have the greatest ability to convince them to take action to reduce global warming.

Yale's research suggests that people, at a baseline, are not talking with each other, not telling their own stories of unsustainability, not talking and listening to people who have differing stories. While there may be talk in social networks, traditional face-to-face encounters are decreasing, and people are not sharing stories about what sustainability means to them, or why it motivates them towards a particular point of view and away from others. Many stories of sustainability are largely held within. From a historical perspective in human history, this is a profound change from our original campfire DNA of telling stories to one another, even if we didn't like each other, or as a community practice in order to learn, adapt and change.

Exercise

- What is your personal story of sustainability?

- What is your story of place, of dwelling?

- What's the story of place surrounding where you work?

- Is there a difference between your organizational story of sustainability and your own story? Do they need to be the same?

- What sustainability story is being told in your change efforts?

- How does your version of the sustainability story end?

From a traditional storyteller's perspective, people might recognize the situation as being stuck in the world of 'Middle Stories' and that there is a need to bring in the 'Big Stories' or the 'Little Stories' as a way to break up and loosen the compaction of narratives found within a story silo.

These are incredibly important findings and should cause any sustainability professional or change agent to ask – *am I telling and listening to stories about change and sustainability within a story silo? What types of stories do I tell or hear told about 'the other'? What stories am I telling about those I'm trying to engage in change work? Do these stories break down story silos or re-circulate narratives within a story silo? How often do I intentionally go listen to and tell stories with people and stakeholders least like myself?*

With growing populations of people self-selecting into story silos there is growing concern that despite all of 'the facts' and the urgency to change, there is a failure of the greater sustainability story. Take for example two recent and broad-reaching Gallop Polls that speak to the impotency of the 'sustainability story' that's being told today. The first[18] revealed that Americans were less concerned about global warming and its effects than they were a few years ago. The second poll,[19] which was conducted in 127 countries, revealed that 38% of the worldwide median population had never even heard about global warming – leaving only 62% of the global population to have reported even hearing about global warming (regardless of whether or not they believe it is happening).

While Yale's findings certainly target an American audience, it's clear the creation of today's story silos is more global by nature and also a phenomenon that is bound to show up within an organization. Questions you should consider include: *What types of story silos exist in my own family, community, organization? Do the six Americas types represent the types of views within my organization or within my stakeholder groups? What are the actual stories being told?*

Why story, why now

In 1936 in Germany, Walter Benjamin, frustrated and fearful of the residual trauma of the First World War, and perhaps foreseeing a second war soon approaching, wrote an essay lamenting what he perceived to be the loss of relevancy of the old forms of storytelling in modern civilization.

As one of the first 'social media' critics of the 20th century, Benjamin argued in his piece 'The Storyteller' that, through the advent of modernization, new technologies have begun to alienate humanity from the histories, memories and mythologies of their communities. This has rendered the power of the greater social narrative, and ultimately the function of the storyteller, irrelevant to modern civilization.

By way of his experience in the war, and having witnessed the disintegration of society, Benjamin believed that without the traditional storyteller our stories no longer served their purpose. The storyteller had served to inspire, advocate, share knowledge for the common good, shine light on the shadows of village life, explore mystery and prepare us in a healthy way for any impending threat, change or future apocalypse. Without the traditional storyteller, the traditional functions of storytelling in the community began to dissolve. This is because, in the old storytelling tradition, the old stories were often told by elders in order to hold institutions and other social structures up to a different light.

He argued that the traditional storyteller held important functions in society, telling the stories of the places and the environments where we lived because our lives were dependent on a story of place and our relationship with each other and the environment. We needed to avoid the tragedy of the commons. Traditionally, the storyteller has held the role as a 'sensemaker' for the commons. Traditionally the storyteller has been the voice to challenge the big stories and act as a conduit for the untold and sometimes untellable stories held in check by the 'Over Culture' of each community,

It's all a question of story. We are in trouble just now because we do not have a good story. We are in between stories. The Old Story – the account of how the world came to be and how we fit into it – is not functioning properly, and we have not learned the New Story. THOMAS BERRY, *THE NEW STORY*[20]

Consequently, stories that previously served to define, inform and interconnect communities with each other soon became more ineffective because of modern technologies. Stories of place used to keep us informed and alive. In more modern times, Benjamin argues that stories and technology have been used to amplify stories about 'the other' and have been used as a symbiotic accelerator for modern warfare, eroding us from our place of dwelling and our traditions of storytelling for meaning making and, ultimately, from each other.

While Benjamin's insights are important, technology has also offered a new and unexpected dimension to storytelling's role in social criticism and change – the campfire has gone digital, slowly erasing the need to be physically in the same place and time to share in the telling of stories. So while we no longer have traditional storytelling communities such as those of Benjamin's era, there is a need for sensemaking through story and storytelling.

Why story, why now? The greatest risk to the sustainability movement may be that today's sustainability stories themselves are 'failing to articulate a vision of a future that is both prosperous while remaining within planetary boundaries', as Joe Cofino of *The Guardian* argues.[21] Why is this? Perhaps we're afraid to truly acknowledge and tell the big stories, to say they matter, or rather, it could be we are just stuck in big story silos unable to see our own blind spots, convinced everyone else doesn't get it. Regardless, I believe it is not just because we need to have a new sustainability story, and acknowledge and name the big stories but we need new storytellers who understand how the storyteller and storytelling operate symbiotically as a deeply human and community-based practice, selflessly acting as a new conduit for imagination, sensemaking and a way forward.

THE FROG PRINCE: PART 2

THE PRINCESS CRIED LOUDER AND LOUDER. She could not console herself over the loss of her golden ball. As she wept, someone called out to her, 'What is the matter with you, princess? Your crying could make the tree weep.'

She looked around to see where the voice was coming from and saw a frog, which had stuck his ugly head out of the water. 'Oh, it's you, old splasher,' she said. 'I am crying because my golden ball has fallen into the deep well.'

'I can help you. I can retrieve your golden ball for you. But what will you give me if I bring back your little treasure?'

'Whatever you want, dear frog,' she said, 'Why, I'll give you my beautiful dress or my pearls and precious stones? No, better yet, I'll give you my golden crown.'

The frog answered, 'I do not want your pearls and precious stones, and as you can see, I have no use for the dress. I don't even want your golden crown. But if you will love me and accept me as your companion, if you will let me sit next to you at your table and eat from your golden plate and drink from your cup and sleep in your bed, then I'll dive deep down and bring your golden ball back to you. Will you will promise this to me?'

'Oh, yes,' said the princess, wiping tears from her eyes, 'I promise if you will just bring the ball back to me.'

The frog was thrilled and immediately dove down into the water. But privately the princess thought, 'What is this stupid frog trying to say? Croak, croak, croak, croak. He cannot be a companion to a human.'

The frog returned a short time later with the golden ball in his mouth and spit it onto the grass. 'Here you are my princess,' he said.

The princess was filled with joy when she saw her beautiful golden ball once again. She picked it up and ran back to the castle, leaving the frog behind. 'Wait, wait,' called the frog, 'Take me along. I cannot hop as fast as you.' But she was long gone. The poor frog was left at the well, alone to croak by himself.

FIGURE 8. The story and shape of The Frog Prince (Act 2).

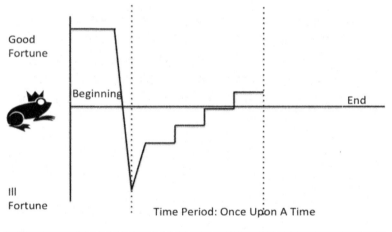

Questions to consider

In telling the sustainability story, I believe our Frog Prince story raises some interesting questions: once we've found our 'bliss', or golden ball, in life what are we willing to do to keep it? Do we remain on top and tell shallow stories, or do we dive deep down into the well, to find the gold, even if it means dealing with unknown stories, unwanted help, ugly partners and inconvenient truths?

In life, and in this story, following one's bliss sometimes intersects with the heroic quests and needs of others, even frogs. We find out that those who we thought of as being good, or chosen like the princess, seem different, more self-serving and less appealing. We learn there are both outer motivations and inner motivations occurring at the same time.

So what is driving this story at this point? Whose story is being told, the princess's or the frog's? Who's the hero? Whose quest are we on? What type of quest? Why do we sometimes reject those who show up to help, even when it's the help we seek? Do you know of any stories in your own life or organizational experience that are similar to some of the themes emerging in this story so far?

CHAPTER 3

The Organization as Storytelling Animal

Middle stories

AT WORK, PEOPLE USE STORY to get buy-in, motivate, engage, set boundaries, spar and deliver threats. Consider when speaking about the return on investment (ROI) for a project, often times the dollar costs of labor can be adjusted to make the case to do a project, but the real value of whether or not to do a project is the story told around why the project is needed rather than manipulated ROI. In this case, it's in the sell, or the art of the tell, which uses the data as a springboard, but not an exact script for how a story is told.

At an organizational level, many approach storytelling from the perspective of 'whoever tells the best story wins'. People are ambitious, passionate about purpose, competitive and wanting to be engaged. The ROI example is just one of the many day-to-day stories told as a form of social currency that impacts organizational performance.

Day-to-day stories at an organization are powerful, impacting morale, employee engagement and general management practices. As storytelling animals, at work we use these stories to curry favor, sweeten the pot, supplicate, cajole or club one another. So there is an important interpersonal dynamic to storytelling, sometimes coming across as acts of macro- or micro-aggressions and macro- or micro-kindnesses. I call these carrot-and-stick stories. Organizations are storied from the inside out as much as from top to bottom. Carrot-and-stick stories are ubiquitous, and in my opinion, part of the inevitable grist of being in a peopled organization.

Platform practice

A great way to practice working with a particular storytelling platform is to challenge yourself to tell one story, the same story, via as many platforms as possible. Try this simple exercise:

First, spend some time thinking about the following question: What is your personal story of sustainability?

Next, try telling your story via as many platforms as possible (you'll have to get creative!):

- Oral story – personal narrative (5 mins) w/ friends or digital recording

- Written story – 250–500 words (blog post, freehand write, etc.)

- Instagram – one image

- Twitter – one Tweet

- Facebook – one Status Update with or without an image

- Digital story/video

- PowerPoint – 5 slides, 5 mins

- Sketch, draw, sculpt or paint – one image

CSR story prompts

When writing sustainability reports and creating other CSR communication pieces, it's always good to remember a few common CSR storylines and plot prompts.

The employee story: Allow the people on the line and in the trenches to tell the sustainability story and convey the employee experience.

Tea company Guayaki does a fantastic job of telling its employee story, and attracting new talent, through stories via info graphics and go-pro style employee-selfie videos.[22] **http://guayaki.com/cebadors.html**

Ethical success stories: Demonstrating the ethics of responsibility, Kosmos Energy had employees from each of their subsidiaries contribute pieces, pictures and personal stories to their CSR report to share in their sense of collective ownership and success.[23] http://www.kosmosenergy.com/responsibility/report/2013/

Stories from your supply chain: Focus on stories of the people and the places in your supply chain. Humanize the people and their relationship with the places found along your value chain. Demystify the linkages. Chicki-fil-a's coffee with a story allows people to meet the farmers and farms.[24] **http://coffeewithastory.chick-fil-a.com/,**

McDonald's provides an excellent example in highlighting people and place through their story of fish supplier, Kenny Longaker.[25] https://www.youtube.com/watch?v=058E2W21WI0

Think about the power and impact of gossip, water-cooler talk or the rumor mill as a form of organizational storytelling. While not necessarily the most esteemed view of storytelling, per se, gossip and rumor mills are excellent examples of the power of story to shape and define organizational culture and social landscapes. We use story to build people and teams up, tear them down, to engage and motivate in order to create boundaries and hierarchy.

At a 'middle story', organizational level, change happens when the stories in an organization are calibrated, or rather woven and perpetually rewoven together. It's what we call aligning strategy. When stories are told well, and coordinated together, at an organizational level, the storytelling helps to communicate, catalyze and calibrate overall group meaning-making, shared vision and purpose. When not told well, or told with ill will, storytelling can distort, blur, isolate, break down or poison organizational meaning-making and employee performance.

The rub at the organizational level of storytelling is how people co-ordinate their individual stories and those told within and around the organizational setting. According to Daniel Pink,[26] people are motivated by autonomy, mastery and purpose. I agree, but at what costs within an organization? How does this show with employees who take this advice of autonomy, mastery and purpose and apply it in maladaptive ways? What about the cult of the individual CEO or C-Suite execs who are out of control with power (think Enron)? What if powerful individuals are so autonomous they use their story to inhibit important organizational stories being told (again, think Enron)?

Carrots and sticks may be dismissed as motivators of the 20th-century organization, but what if they are serving a function? What if carrot-

and-stick stories have both adaptive and maladaptive qualities? What if it is impossible to remove carrots and sticks because they are an organic function of human group dynamics and the role of story in the middle Earth of an organization? I say one must learn to understand the function of carrot-and-stick stories as a natural and predictable part of organizational life. As such, change, influence and performance come from becoming pattern literate to the invisibles of storytelling dynamics.

The function of carrot-and-stick stories

All storytelling has a dynamic tension between the stories lived and the stories told vs the untold – and sometimes untellable – stories of life. There is a Yin–Yang dynamic, or mix of light and shadow in the stories we tell. At an organizational and change level, carrot-and-stick stories are sweet and sour stories that motivate, establish norms and define hierarchical boundaries, influence change and are typically in service to the organizational culture. They can be motivational and be equally de-motivational.

Carrot-and-stick stories are both extrinsic – driven by and telling about external factors – and intrinsic – motivated by internal factors, human potential and other 'invisible' internal narratives.

Carrot-and-stick stories are observable at a 'formal level', 'team-level' of communication and 'oral narrative' level as employee cross-talk and gossip. In becoming mindful of these story patterns, you can become more adept at knowing what's going on within an organization and determining how to influence a healthy balance and mix of carrot-and-stick stories.

- Carrot stories are typically aspirational stories that influence and motivate by way of a particular outcome or reward. Carrot stories can be nourishing, but when told too often, or insincerely, people get sick of eating carrots, lose interest and mistrust them. Consider the carrot story told when Satya Nadella[27] became CEO of Microsoft, when he spoke about his curiosity for learning in his first company-wide email inviting others into this journey as a part of Microsoft's mission.

- Stick stories are stories that are often used as clubs, either to establish power, credibility and dominance or to deliver micro-/macro-aggression and fear. Stick stories can also be stories of structure, boundaries and as tools for growth and discipline. Opposite to their use as clubs, and with the right balance, they can be helpful to defusing tension by way of having healthy and rigorous

Exercise

- Think of a time when you've told a carrot-and-stick story. What was your experience being the storyteller?

- Think of a time when you've been on the receiving end of a carrot or stick story? What's the difference from being a teller?

- What's the right mix of carrot-and-stick story for your organization?

- What mix of carrot-and-stick stories is best for your sustainability efforts?

debate and spurring constructive fights. Consider GM's new CEO, Mary Barra,[28] who publicly fired 15 employees over the cover-up of faulty ignition switches. In this very public firing, the CEO had to acknowledge there was a culture of cover-up. A culture kept in check by stories used as intimidating sticks to keep people silent; now, with this public firing, the story of these firings becomes a new stick of its own, which both resets the organizational cultural story as well as delivers this motivating message to the front line, impacting gossip and water-cooler stories.

Then there's Steve Jobs's famous Stanford graduation speech[29] in which he told three 'carrot & stick' stories which captured the big, middle and little stories of his life – speaking about his own origin story, the second about love and loss with people and organizations, and finally about death and the great mysteries of life. His speech had such power and resonance, as he was able to capture the little, middle, big functions of story and do so by way of a carrot-and-stick mix.

Section takeaways

- We 'make' and 'do' things with story.

- In everyday settings, story is an invisible and powerful force.

- Stories are not always top-down. It is important to consider stories coming from all layers of a company to understand the current voice of the organization.

- Be mindful of how stories are weaving together in an organization – change is truly impactful when there is a conscious intertwining of story at all levels of the organization.

- Stories can be positive or negative and can be used to motivate, provide reward, create boundaries, or impact the chilling effect of certain consequences based on of a story, or 'hypothetical' one.

- Sustainability requires storytelling to utilize not only memory but vision as to the desired future state of the world.

- There is an increase in people telling stories in silos, creating echo chambers and polarizing mono-narratives which impede change.

- In order to make change, sustainability needs to have a cohesive but flexible vision, allowing for variance in viewpoint and context.

THE FROG PRINCE: PART 3

THE NEXT DAY THE PRINCESS sat down at the royal dining table with her father the king. It was a wonderful meal. While she was eating there was a strange knock at the door, and a voice called out, 'Princess, beautiful princess, open the door, please!'

The princess got up from the table and went to see who was outside. She opened the door and there sat the frog, with a grin. Shocked she slammed the door and returned to the table. The king saw she was flustered and asked, 'My child, why are you afraid? Is there a giant outside the door who wants to get you?' 'Oh, no,' she answered. 'It's just a disgusting frog.'

'A frog,' said the king, 'What does the frog want with you?'

'Oh, father,' she said, 'yesterday I went to the great tree that's grown around the well. While I was playing, my golden ball fell into the water. And because I was crying, the frog brought it back up to me if I promised him he could be my companion. But I didn't think that he could leave his water. But now he is just outside the door and wants to come in.'

Then came a second knock at the door, and a voice called out: 'Princess, beautiful princess, open up the door for me. Remember your promise to me? I got your golden ball back.'

The king said, 'If you've made a promise then you must keep it. Go and let the frog in.' The princess went and opened the door, and the frog hopped in and followed her up to her chair.

After she sat down again, he called out, 'Lift me onto your chair and let me sit next to you.' She hesitated – the frog was pretty slimy looking and gross. But the king was watching, so she hesitantly lifted him up.

When the frog was seated next to her he said, 'Now push your golden plate closer, so we can eat together.' She did it and the frog enjoyed his meal, but for her, every bite made her sick to her stomach.

Finally he said, 'I have eaten all I want and am tired. Now please carry me to your room and make your bed so that we can go to sleep.' The princess was disgusted at the idea of the cold, slimy frog in her beautiful, clean bed. Reluctantly, she carried him upstairs, and set him in a corner. Then she got into bed.

The frog hopped up to her and said, 'I am tired, and I want to sleep as comfortably as you do. Pick me up and put me on your pillow or I'll tell your father, the king.'

FIGURE 9. The story and shape of the Frog Prince (Act 3).

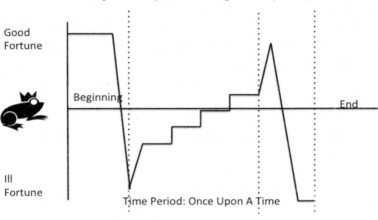

The princess was furious – she had enough with the old splasher. 'You will get your rest, frog,' she said, and the princess picked him up and threw him against the wall as hard as she could. Splat!

Questions to consider

Story exists with a will of its own, and sometimes stories find us and demand we tell them. What frogs show up at your door, warts and all? Consider the story of a whistleblower, or social justice activist, or a social entrepreneur. What do you do with a story once you know about it? Do you run from it or invite it in? There are many stories within the greater sustainability story that are seeking to be told, looking for tellers, and being framed as ugly and unmentionable. You must be brave enough to tell the untold story if it shows up at your doorstep.

Some additional questions:

- Doesn't it seem as if the frog intentionally provokes the princess into hurting him? What are the outer and inner drivers of the story?

- What surprised you about this portion of the story? Is it similar or different to your story?

- Do you feel like the king acts as a moral compass for this story? Is a moral compass an important help? Is this important?

CHAPTER 4

Breaking the Routine: Story as Habit

Stories, urgency and change

ESTABLISHING A SENSE OF URGENCY is often seen as a keystone element for creating change. In story, this urgency translates as the drama and driver of the story. The greater sustainability story has many storylines with many assumed and unexamined drivers and endings. In order to adapt and influence change and direction, we must be able to weave together a collective vision and story of the future that incorporates our own personal storylines of sustainability, as well as the organizational and collective story of what we see sustainability as being and becoming. The sustainability story is, in part, a form of backcasting, where we must develop a shared vision of a future state, or 'future memory', first before we can tell the beginning of the story.

As an example, instead of the stories of quarterly returns (which arguably enables a maladaptive cycle of short-term storytelling) it would be helpful if people and organizations would begin more routinely to tell stories about the type of world we want to live in and leave as a legacy in 20, 50, 100 years or more from now. The time horizons of our stories need to cycle dynamically between the now, the past and the future. Note that this can be done at an organizational and community level as well as on social media. This is a best practice for a healthy community as well as stakeholder engagement.

We need to ask about the stories we are telling that are making our worlds better and worse. What are we making together? How are we taking care of each other and where we live? Who are we listening to who is least like ourselves but may share similar future stories of sustainability, of how it will end?

The irony in asking these questions, of course, is that they may be some of the same types of questions our ancestors have been asking since the dawn of humanity. The same questions which have spurred a multiplicity of sustainability stories, and the same set of questions and stories not shared – stories that remain untold, stories that lead to situations like the Vikings and the Inuit.

Focus your storylines

1. Simplify
2. Keep it real and relatable
3. Avoid cliché
4. Choose your platforms
5. Know your audience

While there is power and potential in the sustainability story, there's an equally important urgency to establish a mindfulness and ethic to the conversation we are having on storytelling. In the modern day, the tricky part in telling the story is in how we individually and collectively envision a similar future state of sustainability in order to establish a shared sense of urgency around the same set of facts, passions and motivators. Story is inherently an invisible force in our everyday. There has to be some form of calibration between stories for alchemy to occur. Besides, it's difficult enough for most people just to agree upon meaning and share the same language and acronyms of sustainability. This is especially true in a global context where the English-language lexicon around sustainability isn't necessarily translatable. More and more, the sustainability debate is no longer about planetary limits, climate science and data – it has instead become a war between differing stories and languages of value, culture and ideology.[30]

Stats vs stories

People ask for data, but believe stories. Why? Because a well-told story can often tell important truths without the use of facts. So why are the facts failing us? Why is there a failure to communicate about the sustainability crisis? Because not everything is storytelling.

Facts and data are important. Yet, communicating about the facts is distinct from telling story. Our modern culture has a bad habit of overly factualizing our stories. Often, well meaning people believe they are actually telling stories, when they are instead just fact telling. This is a maladaptation. Many people think of communicating about the facts and storytelling as being a somewhat synonymous set of methods for transmitting information and knowledge from one person to another.[31]

From this point of view, storytelling is approached as a one-way, unidirectional practice in transmitting facts with meaning. It's about getting MY meanings or MY FACTS into YOUR head. I call this form of communication 'fact telling'. Fact telling is all about the data transfer from me to you, you to me, etc.

Consider how we use the metaphor of 'bullet points': we *shoot* our ideas into another's head. When this transmission approach to communicating the facts doesn't match up with the facts, or go the way we intend, we call it a 'missed message', 'communication breakdown' or just say 'they didn't get it'. If our message doesn't get through, we just reload the facts and fire away again at each other. The end result of our episodes of so-called storytelling becomes louder moments of communication with audiences who are just simply tuning out the uninvited noise.

This transmission or data-transfer model of storytelling emphasizes a communication culture of sound bites, monologues, carefully crafted narratives and talking points. Storytelling, from this perspective, is often about power, control, influence, persuasion, precision and impact. Fact telling creates scenarios where it's often less about winning the argument through the facts, and more about whoever tells the best story, wins. The fields of corporate communications, traditional and social media, marketing, science communication, management consulting and

Don't be such a scientist!

Scientist-turned-film maker, Randy Olson, was asked to speak to the plenary of the first UN Climate Conference on Climate Change Communication in Durban, South Africa on storytelling and change.[32]

Setting the tone for the event, Olson said the only way to tell a good story is to understand the important relationship between the literal (the fact) and the non-literal (the emotion). He believes poor storytellers are those who are too literal-minded and data-oriented. These fact tellers are not as likeable and relatable as those individuals or organizations who can find a voice people can connect with. His most important point: if you want to make change and tell good stories, don't speak like a scientist!

http://www.dontbesuchascientist.com/

employee engagement are just some of the fields where fact telling is part of the lingua franca.[33]

We live in a left-brain culture, which operates from a place of information giving, and a preference for precise, black and white communication. There is nothing wrong with this form of communication, it has its place

---

Statistical numbing – why millions can die and we don't care

Why is it that people can take action to right a specific wrong, or help a specific person, yet grow 'numbly indifferent' when it comes to situations where the person is one victim among many victims?

The answer: statistical numbing.

Particularly fueled through the news media and social media, statistical numbing is interfering with our ability to respond to risk and change says researcher, Paul Slovic,[34] calling this a 'fundamental deficiency in our humanity'. Statistical numbing begins with anything beyond the story of one person, animal, place, etc.

What to do? Remember:

Story of 1 + Data + Image = Influence

As an example, in one study, people were asked how much they would donate to save the lives of children. Those groups introduced to only one child's story and image donated an average of US$11. Groups introduced to the story and image of eight children donated an average of US$5.

---

and relevance, but if you want to tell a story that has resonance or impact, fact telling often becomes a strength overused and a pseudo-satisfier for storytelling.

Fact telling as a form of communication is so ingrained into who we are and how our society communicates, I routinely find clients and other audiences who are just unable to tell a story unless they are fact telling. They think they are telling stories but instead just talk data at people. Examples of the Six Americas and the Story Wars are domains where more people are fact telling at one another, but not necessarily sharing stories, and inspiring mutual understanding and the awareness for change.

The point in making the distinctions between fact telling and storytelling is that they are distinct forms of communication with different functions. A hammer, a saw and a sander are all tools, but we know how and when to use them correctly and incorrectly. With our approach to storytelling and communication we need to know our patterns. Without understanding the distinctions between these forms of communication, people are often applying the wrong tool, at the wrong time, for the wrong audience.

Story selling

As the founder and creative director of LA fashion brand Wren, Melissa Coker knew she had to get the story out about her business. She was on a shoestring budget and had to be creative. In a brilliant move, she commissioned a three-and-a-half minute video, with the goal of telling an authentic story that would be so compelling people couldn't help but talk about it. Ultimately, the story captured the moment of a first kiss between 10 pairs of strangers. This was a shrewd strategy. The 'First Kiss'[35] became a viral YouTube sensation, having now been seen by over

60 million times. People believed in the story, in its innocence, causing a compelling emotional connection to the story. So it was equally jarring to the public audience when it was revealed the story was actually a set up, featuring professionals as a subtle ad for a fashion company. There was a public backlash, viewers felt betrayed, and soon a parody called 'The Slap'[36] began circulating as a very tongue-in-cheek response to 'The First Kiss' which offered a cathartic rebuke for the public being duped, for being treated as if they were stupid.

The ethics of TMI is the future

According to branding and design firm, Landor,[38] Too Much Information (TMI) is the future of sustainability and CSR brand storytelling. 'You cannot get away with bullshit anymore,' says Landor chief strategy officer Thomas Ordahl. People are demanding an ethic of authenticity. Here are three different examples of authentic attempts at sharing a story.

Rose Marcario, CEO & President of Patagonia, penned an open letter about taking part in the People's Climate March:[39] **http://www.thecleanestline.com/2014/09/why-im-joining-the-peoples-climate-march.html**

Responding to negative Twitter comments regarding the McRib, McDonald's Our Food, Your Questions storytelling campaign[40] addresses customers' skepticism head on: **https://www.youtube.com/watch?v=PJoMzhStPNk**

To welcome customers, the CEO of Basecamp[41] tells an inviting and welcoming origin story: **https://basecamp.com/story**

Now despite the blowback and brouhaha over the authenticity of 'The First Kiss', *The Guardian* newspaper[37] declared Melissa Coker's hit 'a lesson in brand strategy', an example of 'the power of great storytelling' where a story could take an audience on a 'feel-good journey'. I have to agree: I believe the video and the strategy behind 'The First Kiss' was brilliant. I respect this work but I wouldn't call it storytelling. I call this story selling. Story selling is a communicative approach intended to persuade, spin and the influence or manipulate behavior. It is manipulated message-making.

Story selling is typically done in the name of selling more stuff, or creating an emotional connection such as a brand relationship. Story selling is found in the fields of marketing, brand communication, advertising, public relations and politics. Story selling seeks to make a brand the hero – or takes the customer on an overly formulaic Hero's Journey adventure. What backfires is when people realize the hero was actually being disingenuous or inauthentic. In reality there's a lot of story selling out there being sold as storytelling – some good, some bad. And, let's face it, story selling works! Yes, it's true – Wren's efforts were even more successful, specifically because of the viral anti-story of 'The Slap'. That's good strategy. The problem is story selling and an anti-story like 'The Slap' often go hand-in-hand.

The way we tell stories creates the primary operating system of our individual, organizational and social worlds. If we fact tell, or story sell, without an ethical or mindful awareness of our communication we may create the blowback pattern I call anti-story. Anti-story is not a story that's 'against' the story told, in a traditional sense, but rather a story told or thought in reaction to being sold an unbelievable or inauthentic story. If the anti-story has been triggered, the story has failed to make its sell. Anti-story is important to listen to as it's like an antibody erupting to counteract a viral attack – in this case, a reaction to viral story selling. As an evolutionary adaptation, anti-story demonstrates how we have become wired to sniff out inauthentic storytelling, because at some point, our lives depended on being aware of story patterns.

Like Wren, Chipotle's animated fresh-food story about the Scarecrow,[42] suffered similar anti-story parodies with 'The Scarecrow the Honest Version'[43] following reports Chipotle actually served GMO burritos.[44]

While the public-at-large may have grown weary or suspicious of the 'story sell', many of the same people also engage in story selling themselves as a primary mode of communication and strategic tactic. This in turn can become a vicious and maladaptive cycle of poor communication, creating mistrust, story silos and echo chambers of anti-story. So while making stories viral has become a widespread strategy, it is ironic that few people ask if their virus of a story is a healthy virus or like the flu.

There are many people and brands out in the marketplace selling the power of story by way of this story seller model. Many people legitimately consider story selling a form of storytelling. I respectfully disagree with this when the primary objective is to sell product, lifestyle and blur the lines between needs and wants, enabling maladaptive practices towards unsustainability. Yet, story selling is a well-worn approach to story and a habit in our cultural business practices. However, I know that when it comes to the context of sustainability, corporate social responsibility and organizational engagement, story selling only leads to problems. Yale's study on the climate change communication confirms that when populations of people feel the stories about climate change are 'spun' or filled with empty buzzwords, superficially it creates distrust, entrenchment and an anti-story about 'the facts' or the sell of the information.

Greenwashing and corporate social responsibility reporting are excellent examples of both the story sell and the anti-story pattern, and a cautionary tale of what happens when you story sell within a space of sustainability. Look at the blowback at BP after it tried to reshape its 'green story', saying BP was an organizational story about going beyond petroleum. Then the Deepwater Horizon event occurred in the Gulf. Oops.

Corporate storytelling is complex. Joel Bakan[45] studies 'The Corporation' as if it was an individual person. In studying the behavior, stories and culture of the legal 'corporate person', Bakan and a team of independent psychologists have routinely witnessed corporate behavior demonstrated to be irresponsible, manipulative, reckless, superficial, narcissistic and grandiose, over-inflating its importance, particularly through the stories it told itself and its stakeholders and customers. Putting this all together, from the perspective of behavioral analysis, the psychologists diagnosed the corporate person as demonstrating psychopathic behavior. Beware: the corporate storyteller may be a psychopath.

I think the conversation on story selling and anti-story is a powerful one to have and to name. Bakan's findings are a clarion call to the potential danger of story selling. Without a mindfulness and ethic of the story selling pattern, one can enable, or contribute to, a superficial set of actions and

> ## CSR without the HR is PR
>
> Corporate Social Responsibility stories **NEED** to amplify the HR:
>
> Human Relationships,
>
> Human Rights and
>
> Human Resourcefulness

stories told, which in the corporate-aggregate, may lead to and enable the psychopathic behavior of the corporation or organization. Story selling is an area of maladaptation that we need to be careful about and keep in balance. I make these distinctions because the marketplace is demanding transparency – people want transparent food labels, supply chains and companies. As consumers of story why wouldn't we want the same transparency from the stories we consume and produce, hear and tell? People don't want to be sold story.

It's important to reiterate: the way that we communicate in story, along with the content of what we say, shapes how we feel about ourselves, the person speaking, and even others who are not in the room. The way we talk 'to, at and with' people creates, sustains and sometimes destroys relationships, organizations, communities and environments. There's nothing wrong with story selling as long as we own it and name it. How we communicate and share our stories of sustainability, therefore, is crucial to making better social and environmental worlds. We need to have ethics in our storytelling and recognize that manipulating each other through forms of inauthentic storytelling is a dead-end path to create forward-looking change.

Creating shared value:
Triple-storyline storytelling

Sustainability and the five big collapse-factor storylines are dynamic and complex as topics. There are an infinite number of stories to be told. Learning how to create shared value through story is not just an important value, but a strategic necessity for any business or NGO that is serious about telling better sustainability stories.

Triple-storyline examples

The Savannah Bee Company offers a great example of character-based triple-storyline storytelling, beginning with the story of the founder and CEO, and his connection to community, nature and place.[46] http://savannahbee.com/; http://vimeo.com/97388791

Ogilvy Rio and Coca-Cola created the 'Every Bottle Has a Story' campaign.[47] http://www.coca-colacompany.com/stories/every-bottle-has-a-story-3-films-bring-to-life-cokes-water-programs

One of the stories features a man from Brazil, who as a child worked as a garbage picker on a landfill site with his mother. Now he runs a project that looks for waste to recycle and employs over 100 people.[48] http://www.wpp.com/sustainabilityreports/2011/the-impact-of-our-work/our-companies/index.html

Exxon Mobile's Life Takes Energy Campaign offers an excellent example of a supply chain storyline that explores the interconnectedness between our individual needs, modern society and sense of place in the story: boiling an egg isn't as simple as just boiling an egg.[49] https://www.youtube.com/watch?v=WrH19H-J4pU

The challenge for the storyteller today is not only knowing the right story to tell, and when to tell it, but also how to assemble the story, choose the platform and be mindful of the many levels, functions and storylines available. What stories will make the most impact: a traditional story, an organizational story or a personal narrative? Which storylines to draw from?

STORYTELLING FOR SUSTAINABILITY:
DEEPENING THE CASE FOR CHANGE

I believe the optimal way to ensure our storytelling is powerful, creating shared value and serving the greater good, is to tell stories that incorporate three important storylines: the 1) storyline of the individual, the person, 2) the storyline of the organization, community or culture, the people, 3) the storyline of the environment and natural living, non-human, world, the place. I call this the triple-storyline model.

Powerful and deep stories are those stories that stack as many storylines together. The triple-storyline model of person, place and people is an easier way to remember and incorporate the five collapse-factor storylines and builds on the power and familiarity of the triple-bottom line approach in business.

Learning to weave all three storylines into the greater narrative of a story allows story to function at multiple levels and not only honor the sustainability story but create a deeper capacity to listen to ourselves, and to others with unbiased, less entrenched ears.

We all understand that in a song we have a melody and harmony. It's a natural part of music. I like to think of the triple-storyline approach to storytelling as similar to music-making. You choose one melodic storyline, such as person, and then build people and place around this primary storyline as harmony lines to your story. How you assemble the melodic and harmonic storylines is really up to you, but you can never have one without the other. Melody and harmony are a natural function of relationship, and so are the storylines of person, people and place.

The triple-storyline approach opens us up to a place within and beneath the habits of our maladaptive storylines and patterns of meaning-making. It opens us up to new ways of storytelling for sustainability.

FIGURE 10. Triple-storyline.

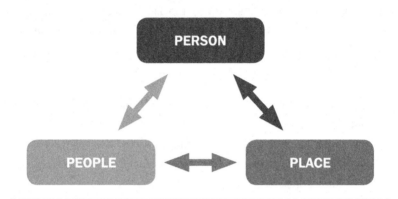

To ensure that our storytelling creates shared value, enabling more authentic meaning-making and culture shift, we must better understand how our individual and organizational stories are to some degree woven together. The triple-storyline approach can help illuminate this so you learn how to better weave webs of connection, instead of tangles and knots.

The triple-storyline model of storytelling is a reminder as much as a source point and heuristic for helping people remember how to craft the most powerful and impactful stories for change. In the upcoming section on making story your own, I will provide an exercise on how to leverage the triple-storyline model for your own storytelling work.

THE FROG PRINCE: PART 4

THE FROG HIT THE WALL WITH A THUD. But when he fell down, the frog transformed into a handsome prince. This changed absolutely everything! He told the princess how a wicked witch had enchanted him, turned him into the frog, and that only the girl of his dreams could have rescued him from the well. The next morning, just as the sun was rising, a carriage pulled up, drawn by eight fine horses with white ostrich feathers on their heads. The young couple woke up, saw the carriage and said good-bye to the king, who was pleased his daughter would marry. At the rear of the carriage stood the young prince's servant, faithful

FIGURE 11. The shape and story of The Frog Prince (Act 4).

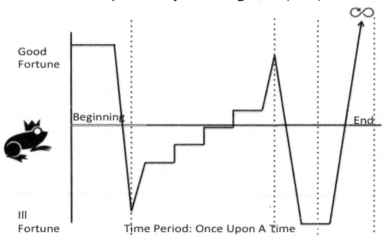

Henry. Henry lifted them both inside and took his place at the rear of the carriage. Off they went. After they had gone a short distance, the prince heard a crack from behind, as though something had broken. He turned around and said: 'Henry, it sounds like the carriage is breaking apart.' 'No, my lord,' answered Henry, 'the carriage is not breaking. That is the sound of the bands that have bound my heart breaking for joy, because you are no longer a frog and are once again a prince.' They safely reached the prince's kingdom and lived happily ever after.

Final reflections

The ending of 'The Frog Prince' is one that often takes people by surprise. What did you notice? Some people realize that the princess is no longer a little girl as she's running off to get married; others respond to how the Frog Prince must have known he would have to seek out his own destruction to be transformed. Others find the servant, faithful Henry, the biggest surprise of the story (even more so when you consider the alternate name for 'The Frog Prince' story is 'Faithful Henry'). Was this story all his dream? Is his faithfulness to the prince, to the dream, to the quest? What stories we are faithful to? Are the faithful heroes, or fools? When we think of sustainability, or unsustainability, which stories do we serve in our telling? Do we have the patience to allow the stories we tell to unfold the way the story genuinely wants to play out? And ultimately, what does 'happily ever after' mean? What does this mean from our perspective of telling the sustainability story: how do we experience the state of bliss of 'happily ever after'? Perhaps the poet Rilke[50] responds to this best in saying sometimes you must 'live the questions and perhaps you will gradually, without noticing it, find yourself experiencing the answers'.

....

CHAPTER 5

Practicing Destiny: What's Your Sustainability Story?

Making story your own: Exercises for practitioners

THIS SECTION IS SET UP to provide a series of hands-on, practical storytelling exercises and skill building practices. These are applicable for individuals, groups and organizations.

Developing your sustainability story

To tell good stories you need to own your own insights and passions. Good storytelling is a discovery process. What are you storytelling for? Once you can

The life of adventure is the quality of life lived in terms of its own inward dynamics. JOSEPH CAMPBELL[51]

answer this question, you need to be able to pivot your story for a variety of situations, platforms and audiences. To develop a flexible and scalable story you need to take the story through three stages of development: 1) the Bones, 2) the Flesh, 3) the Body. Stories need to be flexible, and this three-stage process helps you scale and stretch your story to fit the time, place and setting.

The *Bones* of the story are the basic elements and plotline: Princess drops ball, frog returns ball, etc. Knowing the *Flesh* of the story you are able to stretch the story, adding more description and image; the *Body* of the story is the medium such as oral storytelling, written communication, digital storytelling, organizational storytelling or keynotes, social media, etc.

Bones Exercise 1: Discovering your passionate fact

Individual practice

This is a core practice to get to the heart and core of your story. It is also a practice to help counteract our inner 'fact teller'.

STEP 1: Please consider the following: what is it that drives your work and personal vision in the world. What is your passionate fact? *Note:* This question is more a riddle of 'right-brain passion' + 'left-brain fact', like a Zen Koan. Please feel free to sit with this question.

STEP 2: On one side of a large index card or letter-sized piece of paper, using short keywords, brainstorm ideas or create a word cloud of issues and elements related to your passionate fact.

STEP 3: Once the paper has the keywords of your passionate facts, turn the paper over and draw a picture of your passionate fact. The drawing is not about being perfect, just a visual expression of any form regarding your passionate fact.

STEP 4 – GROUP ADAPTION: Individually complete steps 1–3, and in step 4 everyone in your group should post their drawings on a wall or whiteboard. Individuals should tell the story of the passionate fact picture (which may include their process of drawing the answer). Remind people to tell a story, not get concerned about telling facts about the story.

Bones Exercise Group Adaptation: Discovering your passionate fact

STEP 1: With the whole group together, introduce the question of the passionate fact (see Step 1 above).

STEP 2: For three minutes of silence, have people individually consider the following: *What is it that drives your work and personal vision in the world? What is your passionate fact?*

Note: At an organizational level people can either answer this passionate question from the point of view of the organization or from their own personal point of view as an employee.

STEP 3: Break the group down into small groups of 2–4 people.

STEP 4: Taking turns, have one person tell their passionate fact story to the small group. Listeners should only listen, tellers only tell. No Q&A during the story.

This should be a timed practice as follows: a) for 3 minutes the first storyteller should tell their passionate fact story. When the teller finishes their story, they should remain silent. b) For 3 minutes the listeners have a conversation about the story with each other, as if the teller is not present. c) After the discussion is finished, the teller and listeners thank each other for what they have heard. d) Switch to a new teller, and repeat the same process and continue this process until all individuals have completed their 'telling' rounds.

STEP 5: When everyone has finished have a debrief in the small group about the experience then return to the full group and have a 30-second 'whip around' with each person in the full group sharing their passionate fact story.

Bones Exercise Two: Your convenience story

Individual practice

It's important to carry around a pocket full of stories, ones you can tell at a moment's notice. This is a core practice in learning 'the bones' of your story, a way of learning how to create, recall and tell a short, convenient story. This 'bones' story is typically between 7 and 11 words. The following exercise could be applied to any story; however, for our purposes we're going to continue to develop our passionate fact story (aka your sustainability story).

STEP 1: What is the story of your passionate fact? Either on a computer, smart phone or pen to paper, please write your full story with no fewer than seven words, and no more than 11.

STEP 2: What is the story of the place where your story occurs? Please tell the story of place in no fewer than seven words, and no more than 11. DO NOT include any humans in your story, only environmental setting.

STEP 3: How does your passionate fact story begin? Either on a computer, smart phone or pen to paper, write the opening line to your passionate fact story. This opening line should be no more than 11 words, but could be as simple as one word.

Bones Exercise Group Adaptation: Your convenience story

As a way to develop a shared understanding of a team, or group's understanding of its core sustainability story, the convenience story practice can be adapted as follows:

STEP 1: Working in groups of 2–4 individuals, answer the following in 7–11 words: What is the business or organization's passionate fact story (aka sustainability story)? Have each small group or pair write their story and be prepared to report back and tell their story to the full group. This is best as a timed exercise.

STEP 2: Small groups take turns telling and sharing their 7–11 convenience stories. Groups are encouraged to take notes on themes and storylines that come up.

STEP 3: After listening to the stories, as a group, condense and synthesize the small group stories into one full group story that is no longer than 11 words.

STEP 4: Once the convenience story is agreed upon and written for all to see, ask individuals to consider how they want to share and tell their stories, both their individual and group stories.

Fleshing the Story Exercise 1: What's your storyline?

Individual practice

Because stories are inherently invisible, we need to see what they look like, individually and together. Stories have shapes which can be drawn and fleshed out on a graph. This helps us learn and remember them. The following exercise can be done with any story, including your own sustainability story, or try a carrot-and-stick story. The point with this practice is the more you draw stories you tell and hear, the more you become aware of story patterns and are able to see both maladaptation (such as stories that always end on a down note), or stories which are always overinflated or inauthentic.

FIGURE 12. Shape of story (blank).

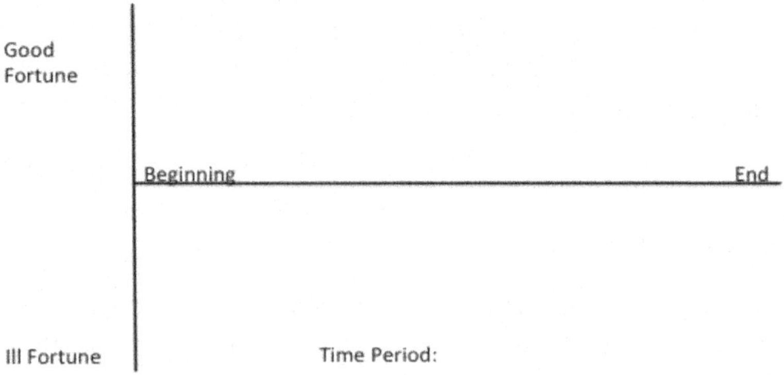

Good
Fortune

Beginning _____ End

Ill Fortune   Time Period:

STEP 1: Draw the following graph with the Good Fortune or Ill Fortune at the top and bottom positions of the vertical line. You can also play with other vertical polarities, such as Sustainable vs Unsustainable, or Carrot or Stick. Be as creative as you want. Bisecting the vertical, in the middle draw a horizontal line running left to right, with a B for beginning and E for End. At the bottom, state the time period, such as 5 years, 1 week, etc. For stories with a non-linear use of time, use 'Once upon a time'.

STEP 2: Ask yourself first, how does your story end? Once you decide this, create an end point dot. For some stories, it may also be appropriate to put an ellipsis '...' or use the infinity symbol to reference that the story somehow continues.

STEP 3: Draw the shape of your story, such as story of sustainability. Start at the beginning and end your storyline by connecting at the end point.

STEP 4 – GROUP ADAPTATION: As a group, walk through the same steps 1–3 together but decide as a group how the shape of the story should begin and end.

Fleshing the Story Exercise 2: Triple storyline map

Group/organizational practice

This exercise is set up so that you can explore the shame of an organization's strategic sustainability story, or that of a particular stakeholder perspective or situation. This exercise can be applied in a variety of ways such as a visioning to flesh out a core sustainability story, or as a stakeholder story analysis or postmortem evaluation of an organization's CSR report. The main point is to give shape to the three storylines of person, people and place.

STEP 1: As a group, or in small groups, draw a Triple Storyline Matrix as above and determine the perspective and voice for each line of the triple storyline – person, people and place.

STEP 2: Ask how does the story end for each storyline – person, people, place? Once you decide this, create an end point dot or symbol.

....

FIGURE 13. Triple bottom line graph example.

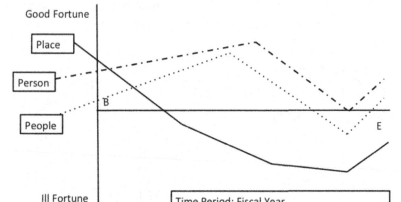

STEP 3: As a group, or in small groups, draw the shape of each story for person, people and place. You should show three distinct storylines with three distinct shapes and beginnings and endings.

STEP 4: As a group, review the different shapes and determine what were important plot points along the shape? What happened when there was a low point or high point? What of the three stories are not necessarily told, and which stories are espoused, but not lived?

Fleshing the Story Exercise 3: Reverse storyboarding

Group/organizational practice

Storyboarding is a popular way of using a frame-by-frame way to mock up a story in images from the beginning to middle to end. This reverse storyboard exercise is different because it asks you to begin with the end vision of your story in mind.

STEP 1: Have your group consider its sustainability story, or a vision of where the organization wants to be in, for example, 5 years.

Triple Storyline Matrix

STORYLINE	POSSIBLE PERSPECTIVES	
Place	Environment	Industry
People	Employees	Stakeholder groups (internal and external)
Person	Employee	Stakeholder (internal and external)

STEP 2: In your future story, imagine the story of place in the future.

STEP 3: Draw six boxes forming a grid on flip chart paper. A storyboard has 5 boxes/frames + 1 box/frame for THE catalyzing moment in your future story.

....

FIGURE 14. Reverse storyboard.

STEP 4: Starting from the last frame of your story (bottom right), work backwards to tell your story by visually drawing out or mocking up the story.

STEP 5: Debrief – talk about the experience and tell your story.

STEP 6 – GROUP ADAPTATION: Break into small groups of between 2 and 4 people and have each group create their own storyboard following the same process as above.

STEP 7 – GROUP ADAPTATION: At some point, have individuals within the small groups move to another group to help. This is similar to a World Café, where people rotate from group to group, leaving a core storyteller with each storyboard.

Story Function – Body Exercise: What's the body of my story?

Individual/group practice

This is a practice to get into the three levels of your sustainability story, and create a sturdy outline for you to build upon. I like to approach this as if I'm having an interview or Q&A session with each storyline of my story. These stories can be true to life, fictional or factional. Regardless, you need to imagine the point of view for each storyline – the little/person, middle/people and big/place of your story. With place, imagine it and personify it in your Q&A. Please use the following matrix as a guide.

You should answer the following 12 questions per storyline and POV, telling the story from each point of view – big, middle and little. When you have finished this process, answer question 13 – what's the red thread, the one element that ties these three levels of story together?

HUMAN HIERARCHY OF STORIES	WHAT'S THE STORYLINE?	TRIPLE STORY LINE LEVEL
Big story	What's the storyline and POV?	Place, environmental, deep ecology, the wild

STORYTELLING FOR SUSTAINABILITY:
DEEPENING THE CASE FOR CHANGE

Middle story	What's the storyline and POV?	People, organizational, community, political she, he, we, us
Little story	What's the storyline and POV	I am, me, and the hero within

1. Who are you?

2. Where's home?

3. What do you remember before the actual story begins?

4. When does your story begin?

5. Where does your story begin?

6. Who's in your story?

7. What is your golden ball?

8. What do you quest for? Why is this urgent?

9. What or who is your monster?

10. What's your catalyzing moment?

11. Is there resolution?

12. How do you return to home? How does this story end?

13. What's the red thread between the three levels of story? What ties this together?

References

1. http://storyofstuff.org

2. Indian proverb.

3. Seal, G. 2001. *Encyclopedia of Folk Heroes* (Santa Barbara, CA: ABC-CLIO).

4. Campbell, J. 2008. *The Hero with a Thousand Faces*. Bollingen Series, 3rd edn (Novato, CA: New World Library).

5. McCole, J. 1993. *Walter Benjamin and the Antinomies of Tradition* (Ithaca, NY: Cornell University Press).

6. http://www.youtube.com/watch?v=oP3c1h8v2ZQ

7. http://www.jcf.org

8. Campbell, J. 2004. *Pathways to Bliss: Mythology and Personal Transformation* (Novato, CA: New World Library).

9. http://www.wernerherzog.com

10. Diamond, J. 2005. *Collapse: How Societies Choose to Fail or Succeed* (London: Penguin).

11. http://en.wikipedia.org/wiki/Our_Common_Future

12. Kristof, Nicholas D. and Sheryl WuDunn, 2009. *Half the Sky: Turning Oppression into Opportunity for Women Worldwide* (New York: Random House).

13. http://www.halftheskymovement.org

14. http://environment.yale.edu/climate-communication/

15. http://environment.yale.edu/climate-communication/files/Six-Americas-September-2012.pdf

REFERENCES

16. http://www.poetryfoundation.org/bio/muriel-rukeyser

17. http://environment.yale.edu/climate-communication/article/how-americans-communicate-about-global-warming-april-2013/

18. http://www.gallup.com/poll/146606/Co...er-Levels.aspx

19. http://www.gallup.com/poll/117772/Awareness-Opinions-Global-Warming-Vary-Worldwide.aspx

20. Berry, T. 1978. The new story: Comments on the origin, identification and transmission of values. *Teilhard Studies* (#1, Winter).

21. http://www.theguardian.com/sustainable-business/sustainability-movement-fail-future

22. http://guayaki.com/cebadors.html

23. http://www.kosmosenergy.com/responsibility/report/2013/

24. http://coffeewithastory.chick-fil-a.com/,

25. https://www.youtube.com/watch?v=058E2W21WI0

26. http://www.danpink.com

27. http://news.microsoft.com/2014/02/04/satya-nadella-email-to-employees-on-first-day-as-ceo/)

28. http://www.washingtonpost.com/business/economy/gm-ceo-15-fired-over-ignition-switch-recalls-probe-shows-pattern-of-failures-no-coverup/2014/06/05/2dc575bc-ecb8-11e3-9f5c-9075d5508f0a_story.html

29. http://news.stanford.edu/news/2005/june15/jobs-061505.html

30. http://www.ssireview.org/articles/entry/climate_science_as_culture_wa

31. http://www.iied.org/tweet-tweet-cop17-climate-communications-day

32. http://www.dontbesuchascientist.com/

33. http://bigthink.com/risk-reason-and-reality/statistical-numbing-why-millions-can-die-and-we-dont-care

34. http://www.sas.upenn.edu/%7Ebaron/journal/7303a/jdm7303a.htm

35. https://www.youtube.com/watch?v=IpbDHxCV29A

36. https://www.youtube.com/watch?v=ninOz5ValUM

37. http://www.theguardian.com/media-network/partner-zone-brand-union/wren-first-kiss-melissa-coker-brands

38. http://landor.com/pdfs/Trends%202015_19Nov2014.pdf?utm_campaign=PDFDownloads&utm_medium=web&utm_source=web

39. http://www.thecleanestline.com/2014/09/why-im-joining-the-peoples-climate-march.html

40. https://www.youtube.com/watch?v=PJoMzhStPNk

41. https://basecamp.com/story

42. https://www.youtube.com/watch?v=IUtnas5ScSE

43. https://www.youtube.com/watch?v=nYZgWYZIAZU

44. http://www.businessweek.com/articles/2013-06-18/the-genetically-modified-burrito-chipotle-tells-all)

45. http://www.thecorporation.com/

46. http://vimeo.com/97388791

47. http://www.coca-colacompany.com/stories/every-bottle-has-a-story-3-films-bring-to-life-cokes-water-programs

48. http://www.wpp.com/sustainabilityreports/2011/the-impact-of-our-work/our-companies/index.html

49. https://www.youtube.com/watch?v=WrH19H-J4pU

REFERENCES

50. Rilke, R. 1993. *Letters to a Young Poet*, in an edition by M.D. Herter Norton (translator) (New York: W.W. Norton & Co.).

51. Svehla, C. 2010. *Blisters on the Way to Bliss* (Santa Barbara, CA: Opus Archives and Joseph Campbell Foundation).

52. Sachs, J. 2012. *Winning the Story Wars: Why Those Who Tell – and Live – the Best Stories Will Rule the Future* (Boston, MA: Harvard Business School Publishing).

53. http://www.fastcodesign.com/3038951/tmi-is-the-future-of-branding

Image Credits

 'Frog', designed by Brianna Reed, sourced from thenounproject. com: http://thenounproject.com/term/frog/34881/

'Crown', designed by Ben Rex Furneaux, sourced from the nounproject.com: http://thenounproject.com/term/crown/ 3677/

 'Environment', designed by OCHA Visual Information Unit, sourced from thenounproject.com: http://thenounproject. com/term/environment/4223/

 'Kayak', designed by Gabriele Malaspina, sourced from thenoun project.com: http://thenounproject.com/term/kayak/17483/

 'Viking Hat', Public Domain, sourced from thenounproject. com: http://thenounproject.com/term/viking/3219/

 'Friends', designed by Arthur Shlain, sourced from the nounproject.com: http://thenounproject.com/term/friends/ 60849/

Printed in the United States
by Baker & Taylor Publisher Services